TUBAFEST
Celebration Fanfare

Husa

* Tuba 1 and 2 parts may be played on Euphonium

AMP8265

★ Tuba 1

TUBAFEST
Celebration Fanfare

Karel Husa

* Part may be played on Euphonium.

AMP8265

★ Tuba 2

TUBAFEST
Celebration Fanfare

Karel Husa

* Part may be played on Euphonium.

AMP8265

Tuba 3

TUBAFEST
Celebration Fanfare

Karel Husa

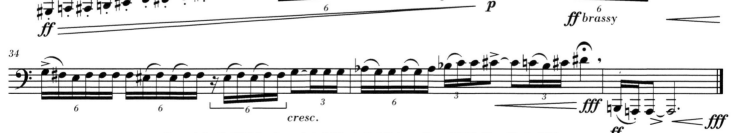

AMP8265

Tuba 4

TUBAFEST
Celebration Fanfare

Karel Husa

AMP8265